T0193400

Walking
through the
Valley

My Journey through Sickness

Tenssie V. Ramsay

authorHOUSE®

AuthorHouse™
1663 Liberty Drive
Bloomington, IN 47403
www.authorhouse.com
Phone: 833-262-8899

Published by AuthorHouse 07/13/2023

ISBN: 979-8-8230-1164-8 (sc)
ISBN: 979-8-8230-1165-5 (e)

Library of Congress Control Number: 2023913049

Print information available on the last page.

Scripture quotations marked KJV are from the Holy Bible, King James Version (Authorized Version). First published in 1611. Quoted from the KJV Classic Reference Bible, Copyright © 1983 by The Zondervan Corporation.

DEDICATION

This book is dedicated to my family, who
exhibited patience and cared for me,

and to

all the people of God who continually lifted
me up in their prayers during my sickness.

Surely he hath borne our griefs, and carried our sorrows: yet we did esteem him stricken, smitten of God, and afflicted. But he was wounded for our transgressions, he was bruised for our iniquities: the chastisement of our peace was upon him; and with his stripes we are healed.

— Isaiah 53:4–5 (KJV)

CONTENTS

ACKNOWLEDGMENTS

I must first honor God, who is the head of my life and the one who kept my mind calm during my months of sickness. God comforted and ministered to me daily. He fed me spiritual food when the natural food could not go down my throat. God granted me favor from the very first day that I entered the hospital. I received the best care from the phenomenal, caring nursing team, who sometimes went beyond the call of duty to take care of my needs.

I offer special thanks to the members of my family who stood by me, changed their work schedules, spent time in the hospital room with me, and prayed for me without ceasing. If I should try to name everyone who played a part in my recovery, some folks would be upset as I would probably forget to name them.

However, I would be remiss if I didn't highlight some pastors and their congregations who played an integral part in my recovery, as they spearheaded corporate prayers and fasting on my behalf: my spiritual leader, Bishop Arthur Thomas of the Oneness Rehoboth Apostolic Church; Pastor Victor Nyarko of the Victory Family Worship Center; Bishop Baron Simmonds of Spicey Grove

Pentecostal in St. Ann, Jamaica; Pastor Winston Nelson of Lime Walk Pentecostal in Jamaica; Bishop Courtney Golding of Orangefield Pentecostal in Jamaica; Bishop Frank Otto of the Linstead Pentecostal Tabernacle; and a host of other friends and saints of God.

Thanks for your support and encouragement to me and my family. Your diligence has not gone unnoticed; your reward is from the Lord Jesus Christ.

Additionally, a special thank you to Dr. Victor T. Nyarko and Mrs. Mary E. Simmonds, who took the time to proofread my book at no cost to me. I appreciate their honest feedback and input in helping me accomplish my dream.

INTRODUCTION

This book, *Walking through the Valley*, was birthed from my innermost being one night when I woke up suddenly because of pain. I lay on the bed looking up at the ceiling, with tears streaming from my eyes, and asked God what lesson he was teaching me through this sickness. Suddenly, in the stillness of the night, I heard these words: "Document your story so others can read and be encouraged." This directive was given approximately one month after my surgery.

I could hardly wait for daylight to come so I could share with my daughter what had happened and ask her to get me my laptop so I could start writing my story. My daughter became excited but was concerned about whether I was strong enough to sit up for any length of time. I felt confident that God would give me strength as he was the one who had instructed me to write. I began to write about my sickness, and the words literally flowed freely from my heart to be transcribed right before my very eyes.

A few days later, I had written only the first paragraph of my story when my condition worsened. So I placed my writing on hold until I was strong enough to continue. It is my hope and prayer that, after reading this book, your faith will increase and you will have confidence in the fact that there is nothing too hard for God to do. God's promises are sure, and he will never go back on his word.

I recall quite vividly the words of a dynamic preacher as he impressed upon the congregation the importance of prayer and why we should never stop praying. The minister stated that, when we pray, our prayers are stored and are made available in moments when we are unable to pray. I went through those moments, and I thank God that I knew how to pray and had some prayers stored up for those rainy days. Let's always find the time to pray because prayer is the key that unlocks every closed door.

> Praying always with all prayer and supplication in the Spirit, and watching thereunto with all perseverance and supplication for all saints. (Ephesians 6:18)

CHAPTER 1

The Journey Begins

My daughter and I arrived at the designated hospital, and after completing the check-in process, we were directed to the third floor, the preoperative holding area, where I received information from the operating room (OR) staff and signed the necessary paperwork. Although it was wintertime, it was a beautiful Monday morning, and I felt confident that I would be in and out of surgery in a timely manner. The operating team of surgeons came to provide detailed information about the surgery, including the anticipated recovery time.

The team gave me the opportunity to ask questions, then the process began. They connected me to an intravenous (IV) pole holding bags of IV fluids. A member of the operating team narrated every step of the process, but I cannot recall most of what was said during the few minutes before my surgery because I was busy praying that everything would work in my favor and that I would have a successful surgery.

The waiting seemed never-ending, and I became restless. My daughter reassured me that everything would be okay because she was in constant contact with the operating team while we waited in the preoperative holding area. Time seemed to have slowed down, and I wondered for a moment if the time for my surgery had been changed. My daughter kept talking to me and ignoring my repeated question: "What's taking them so long?" She would introduce random topics to shift my focus, and I said, "Okay, I got it! I see what you are doing, and I thank you."

It seemed as if we had waited for hours when, in fact, it was less than half an hour. My daughter played a very important role during the preoperative process by acting as my advocate. She observed everything that was done to me and asked questions. I felt so proud of her, and I whispered a prayer to God on her behalf.

The time came when my daughter and I had to part company as I was being rolled down the hallway to the OR. I smiled and said to her, "See you later." I arrived in the OR, which was a very large and sterile room that was freezing, and began to shiver. The medical team made me very comfortable and kept talking to me in a calm manner.

The anesthesiologist came to my side and, with the most winning smile, explained her role and what she was about to do. She stated, "I am about to apply the anesthesia, and you are going to feel a little sting, and then …" I didn't hear the rest. I was out.

I woke up hours later and realized I was in the recovery room being questioned by nurses to verify my orientation.

I must have given the right answers because I was whisked to the sixth floor, where I would stay overnight. I was still drowsy, so nothing really mattered to me. I lost track of time as I fell in and out of sleep. It was the sound of my daughter's voice that woke me up, and I glanced at the clock in the room and saw the time.

I thought, *I must have been tired to have slept for so long.* My daughter was talking to the nurse outside my door in very low tones, almost like she was whispering. For a moment there, I wondered why she was whispering, then I thought, *The nurse might have told her I was still sleeping.*

I was now wide awake and waited excitedly for my daughter to enter the room. I was pleasantly surprised when she did because she was not alone. She was accompanied by my youngest son, who brought me a beautiful teddy bear dressed in a red shirt with the words "Feel better" across its chest. He also brought me a warming pad—so sweet and thoughtful.

I thought I would be spending the night alone in that hospital room, but my daughter thought better, as she had not been pleased with the treatment I had gotten on the sixth floor. The night was uneventful because she was with me. I was happy to be discharged the following afternoon, and my daughter and I headed home.

When I got home, I was pleasantly surprised to see the work that had been put in place to make my living environment more comfortable. My children had rearranged some furniture and transformed the area where I would be spending most of time during my recuperation. I was touched by their kind gesture and insight as to what I would need postsurgery.

I pause to give God thanks for my children; because of their proactivity, my transition from the hospital to home was seamless. The word of God endorses good children like mine, and in the psalms, David captured this beautifully:

> Lo, children are an heritage of the LORD: AND THE FRUIT OF THE WOMB IS HIS REWARD. (PSALM 127:3 KING JAMES VERSION, OR KJV)

CHAPTER 2

Postsurgery Recovery

During the first week home, I spent most of my days sleeping as I was very lethargic. I was discharged with a puree diet order, and this was not very appetizing. My family did all they could to be creative and make mealtime a pleasure for me. It was challenging for them as well because there were times when they spent hours in the kitchen preparing my prescribed meal, but when they presented it to me, I would just look at it and say, "I can't eat that."

I tried very hard to please my family by sometimes forcing myself to eat, but I would become nauseated and have trouble swallowing the food. This usually left me feeling drained and exhausted, and I would eventually fall asleep.

One day the pain was so excruciating that I cried out, "Lord, please let someone be praying for me!" After uttering those words, I heard, "What time I am afraid, I will trust in thee" (Psalm 56:3 KJV). I kept repeating the words until I felt calm. After a while, I looked at my phone and saw that a dear friend had left me a voice message, and when I played it, I began to cry. She was praying for me, and the prayer was direct. You see, Jesus promised that he would never leave us alone, and David captures it well: "Yea, though I walk through the valley of the shadow of death, I will fear no evil: for thou are with me; Thy rod and thy staff they comfort me" (Psalm 23:4 KJV).

Toward the end of week two, I had another experience where I was in so much pain that I didn't know what to do, and I picked up my phone and dialed my spiritual mother and mentor in Jamaica. Without asking what was wrong, she began to pray, and indeed she touched heaven because I felt instant relief. I continued having unbearable pain on some days; however, I had a few good days.

While going through those trying days, I sometimes recalled this line from a song: "I am a new creation no more in condemnation here in the grace of God I stand." The song became alive in my thoughts as I pictured the group of children dubbed the Rising Stars singing in their church in Hackney, England.

CHAPTER 3

Postsurgery Appointment

I attended my postsurgery appointment, and the doctor gave me a clean bill of health along with a list of dos and don'ts. I felt relieved as I graduated to a soft-food diet, and I began to plan my menu. This was short-lived, though, as I began spiraling down. It was difficult to swallow, and I kept feeling as if my breathing was about to stop at any moment. I had to return to the hospital, where doctors did a series of tests and decided to revisit the surgery site.

I had mixed feelings as I listened to the surgeon say, "We should be able to fix the problem with another procedure." The trajectory of my life seemed to have changed overnight. I was no longer able to consume the puree diet and only took sips of water daily.

There were days when I became very hungry and would repeat these words: "Remove far from me vanity and lies: Give me neither poverty nor riches; Feed me with food convenient for me" (Proverbs 30:8). My body would then calm down, and I would fall asleep. When I woke up, I would feel like I had just had a three-course meal.

My new norm was restless and sleepless nights, nausea, my body's rejection of all forms of nutrition, and difficulty swallowing. Psalm 23 became real and alive for me, and I felt like I was in verses 1 and 2: "The Lord is my shepherd I shall not want. He maketh me to lie down in green pastures: He leadeth me beside the still waters" (Psalm 23:1–2 KJV). I personalized the psalm, and I felt like I owned it. I kept repeating the words as I encouraged myself. Then I went off to the hospital again for an IV infusion (for dehydration) and two hours of IV therapy.

My brother and sister-in-law held impromptu prayer meetings via telephone on a nightly basis. I was encouraged by the outpouring of love from my church family as well as my immediate family. I learned that folks all around the globe were praying for me.

My brother-in-law and brother summoned their congregations to fast and pray for my healing. I was encouraged as brethren and friends, both local and abroad, sent daily texts with words of encouragement and prayers.

My ability to communicate became affected, as my body no longer responded to external prompts. Now I needed the Lord Jesus to restore my soul. "He restoreth my soul: He leadeth me in the paths of righteousness for his name's sake" (Psalm 23:3).

CHAPTER 4

Complications

On December 13, 2022, I had to return to the hospital for another IV infusion and a follow-up procedure based on the results of the swallowing evaluation and CT scan done earlier. I returned home the following day and thought, *This has to be it.* I had no idea that I was about to go through some more tests. At this point in my life, I was determined to continue giving God thanks and maintain a positive attitude.

Some days I felt my strength returning, while on other days I felt listless, helpless, and confused. *What is happening to me, dear God?* I wondered. *When will I get well? Are you hearing the cry of the many people who are interceding for me? Are you even hearing my cry?* I kept reflecting on a song that I recalled from my childhood days while growing up in Jamaica.

About a year earlier, I had dissected the song as I led a prayer group. The song says, "Will you be true, will you be true when the time of testing comes, and Jesus calls on you? Will you be true, will you be true, or will you turn and run away as the cowards do?" I remembered the intensity with which I had spoken that morning, and I pleaded with my fellow brothers and sisters to remain true to God even in adverse situations.

Then, I pondered the questions, *Is this the time of my testing? How will I maneuver this phase of life? Will I continue to trust God, or will I portray a defeatist attitude?*

> Then Satan answered the Lord, and said, Doth Job fear God for nought? Hast not thou made a hedge about him, and about his house, and about all that he hath on every side? Thou hast blessed the work of his hands, and his substance is increased in the land. But put forth thine hand now, and touch all that he hath, and he will curse thee to thy face. (Job 1:9–11 KJV)

Job lost everything that he possessed, and the scripture states, "Then Job arose, rent his mantle and shaved his head, and fell down upon the ground and worshipped." How can we worship when we have lost all that we have? God gave Satan permission to touch Job but only with a stipulation: "And the Lord said unto Satan, Behold, he is in thine hand; but save his life" (Job 2:6).

CHAPTER 5

The Tides Are Turning

Jesus, I need you more than ever before, I prayed silently, *and it seems as if my body is deteriorating before my very eyes. Jesus, I am weak. Help me, save me, renew my strength because I can't go on without you.* My family was very concerned about my health, and my older sister felt compelled to be with me during my sickness. She flew in from Jamaica to give support and help with my care.

This seemed to be the tumultuous stage of my sickness journey. I was on a rocky road with pains racking my body, constant feelings of nausea, difficulty swallowing and breathing, and the list goes on. There were times when I didn't know if it was night or day because they all seemed the same to me. The symptoms were as real as the concerns.

"So went Satan forth from the presence of the Lord, and smote Job with sore boils from the sole of his foot unto his crown unto his crown" (Job 2:7). My illness was not sore boils; however, I was experiencing excruciating pain all over my body. And by this time, I was imagining how Job must have felt when he was sick. I became very weak and could not move around without the physical support of my family. The fight was on, and it was real! It had become warfare, and I knew I must fight. I must stand on the words of God because his promises are sure.

As I grew weaker each day, I sometimes prayed quietly in my mind, questioned God about my sickness, and requested that he give me a timeline. During those moments, God reminded me that his timing and that of humans are not the same. I changed my prayer and asked God to forgive me for thinking the way I had. I was reminded that God is always on time.

Life is filled with challenges, and I realize that everyone has tests to endure in order to be victorious. Job was not the only person in the Bible who went through hard times. Jeremiah the prophet was faced with challenges of a different nature. As I thought about the Bible's account of Jeremiah's dilemma, I became more aware that our life experiences, traumas, setbacks, illnesses, and challenges are stepping stones to a closer walk with God.

I tried to imagine how Jeremiah must have felt when he was thrown into a dungeon that had no water. I wondered if at any time he felt hopeless, helpless, or angry with God. "Then took they Jeremiah and cast him into the dungeon of Malchiah the son of Hammelech, that was in the court of the prison, and they let down Jeremiah with cords. And in the dungeon, there was no water, but mire so Jeremiah sunk in the mire" (Jeremiah 38:6 KJV).

On December 31, 2022, I was again having difficulties breathing and swallowing. I contacted the on-call nursing service and explained what was happening to me. The nurse contacted the surgeon, who suggested that I go to the emergency room (ER) for medical attention. My husband and my sister took me in.

I tried to analyze the looks on the medical workers' faces as I was whisked through the initial process and waited to be assigned a room. I could hardly hold my head up for long periods of time and kept resting on my sister's shoulder. They gave me IV fluids and did a full blood work test and a CT scan. After all medical protocols were completed, the doctors decided to admit me to the hospital once again.

My sister sat with me and massaged my back while praying earnestly to God on my behalf. She texted other family members, including her family in Jamaica, and told them of my readmittance and asked that they pray. Much later that night, before midnight, my daughter relieved my sister and obtained permission to spend the night in the hospital room with me.

Traditionally everyone makes plans for end-of-year celebrations. Some folks usher in the new year at parties, at Times Square to see the ball drop, or in church. The last was always my choice, but there I was on December 31, 2022, admitted to the hospital. As I watched the service at my church via live stream, I whispered these words to my daughter: "Who would have thought that I would be spending New Year's Eve in a hospital?" My daughter calmly said, "Mom, don't worry about it! God's got you."

Then she added that she had called my close friend who is a prayer warrior and that she was praying for me as we spoke.

I felt calm and was thinking, *It does not matter what takes place in this leg of the sickness journey; I know for sure that God has not changed, and his promises are sure.* I began to praise and thank God for life because, after all, if we are following the statutes and principles of the gospel, we should be thankful in any and every situation or circumstance. The scripture supports having the right attitude in this verse: "In everything give thanks: for this is the will of God in Christ Jesus concerning you" (1 Thessalonians 5:18).

CHAPTER 6

Dawn of a New Year

On January 3, 2023, I was back in the OR as there had been no changes in my symptoms. The surgeon had stated, "We need to try something else to help you as nothing that was done prior to this time seems to have helped." He outlined the procedure, adding that there were some risk factors involved, as in all procedures. My family and I were faced with the daunting task of deciding whether I should be subjected to another procedure.

We all decided that, if it meant good results, then the surgeon should proceed with the procedure. My sister laid her hands on me and prayed a powerful prayer asking God to protect me and for there to be no complications. As I was wheeled from the room, I took a last look at my sister and said, "See you soon."

By then I was accustomed to the preoperation procedures and jargon used by the medical team. Of course, the team had to maintain protocol and professionalism, so they outlined the procedure step by step and gave me the relevant paperwork to sign. I thought, *I hope this is the last time I'll ever have to sign paperwork for any procedures or surgery.* The procedure was completed quickly, and I began waiting patiently to return to my norm.

I was falling in and out of sleep, and in my mind, I could hear this beautiful song being sung in my pastor's voice:

> I trust in God wherever I may be, upon
> the land or on the rolling sea, for, comes
> what may, from day to day, my heavenly
> Father watches over me.
>
> I trust in God I know he cares for me,
> on mountain bleak, or on the stormy sea;
> Though billows roll, He keeps my soul,
> my heavenly Father watches over me.

My daughter was the first familiar face I saw in the recovery room when I opened my eyes. I was kept in the recovery room and monitored for a while until I became stable. I thought about my sister, who was waiting in my hospital room, and I knew she spent the time praying for me. I fell asleep again with the comforting thought that God was in charge and I was safe and secure in his arms.

The weeks following that procedure seemed to go by in slow motion. My sister and daughter took turns at the hospital, covering both day and night shifts as they watched and prayed for a miracle to take place. They took turns reading and responding to text messages on my behalf and answering phone calls as I was too weak to even hold my phone to my ears. The reminder that prayers were going up for me gave me a feeling of security and hope. "And this is the confidence that we have in him, that if we ask anything according to his will, he heareth us" (1 John 5:14).

My days and nights that were interspersed with "I am going to take your vitals now," "I need to draw some blood," "I have an injection for you," "A new order was sent by your doctor for this medication," "We can't find your veins, so let's get the vein finder," and then "The vein finder did not work, so the IV team had to be called." The blood-test results were not looking good and, at this point, decisions had to be made in a timely manner.

There were more questions than answers, and the surgery team had to make the final call. The blood-test results were not good, and even though they were repeated at different times of the day, nothing had changed. My body was not receiving the essential nutrients needed for full functioning. I was losing weight rapidly, my digestive system was not working, my heart rhythm was abnormal, and I was experiencing muscle weakness.

My potassium level was extremely low, and my doctors decided to administer intravenous potassium. It was infused on a twenty-four-hour basis, and I was closely monitored for any signs of irritation. After two days of infusion, I started experiencing a burning sensation under my skin, my entire right arm was swollen and discolored, and I was in pain. This was brought to the attention of the nurse, and she contacted the doctor.

They disconnected the intravenous potassium and later discontinued it. My health, however, continued to worsen, and this was of concern not only to my family but also to the medical staff. The surgeon communicated his concerns about my failing health to me and my family members, and the decision was made to help provide nutrients to my body intravenously.

The nurse came to my room to prepare me for the total parenteral nutrition (TPN) connection. He provided the information I needed and was able to answer all my questions and concerns. The sterile process lasted about an hour. During this time, only the two nurses were in my room, and a stop sign was placed on my door.

This all took place around the time when my sister normally came in to start her routine daily visit with me. She shared with me afterward the fear she felt when she saw the stop sign on my door. But the nurse manager assured my sister that all was well and that she would be allowed in the room when the procedure was completed.

After the TPN was put in place, I wondered briefly if that would be my new normal. My prayers became more intense and direct as I asked the Lord Jesus to give me an appetite and allow me to eat regular food with no complications so I could be removed from the TPN feeding.

The nursing staff closely monitored the TPN as the line and bag had to be changed every twenty-four hours. I would watch the nurses as they changed the bag and line, and sometimes I would question them as to whether they knew the timeline for the TPN. They would answer my question by saying either "Who knows?" or "Only time can tell!" Those answers were not very encouraging, but I kept praying that the TPN was only a temporary fix.

The surgeon came to my room after I had been on the TPN for a few days and had several blood tests, and he had a look of hopelessness in his eyes. I looked at him nervously and, in my mind, I was trying to rationalize the reason for that look on his face. I thought that something must be seriously wrong with me and he was trying to figure out how best to break the news to me.

After the surgeon made his preliminary greetings, including asking me how I felt, he stated, "I wish there was something else I could do for you. I have tried everything possible, and nothing seems to work. I am sorry." I looked him square in the eyes and with confidence stated, "Doctor, you have done all that you possibly can for me, and I don't blame you because you are human. And now the rest is up to God."

The doctor's mood literally changed before me, and it seemed as if a weight had been lifted off his shoulders. He then looked at my sister and said, "Do you have any questions for me?" She replied, "Doctor, my sister said it all—the rest is now up to God." You see, I validated the doctor's feelings and affirmed that he was human and that my God is the surgeon of all surgeons. Once we accept our limitations as humans and allow God to take his rightful place, we will get positive results. At that moment in time, I remembered the scripture "For thou shalt worship no other god: for the Lord, whose name is Jealous, is a jealous God" (Exodus 34:14).

CHAPTER 7

I Trust in God

> No weapon that is formed against thee
> shall prosper; and every tongue that
> shall rise against thee in judgment thou
> shalt condemn. This is the heritage
> of the servants of the Lord, and their
> righteousness is of me, saith the Lord.
> (Isaiah 54:17)

This verse was quoted to me repeatedly through prayer
and encouragement from family and friends. I fell asleep
knowing that God is in charge and I can rest in him. I had
a dream that confirmed that I was going through warfare.
I won the battle when I called out to Jesus for help, and I
woke up feeling victorious.

For us to fight the enemy, we must have a personal
relationship with God. We should seek a friend before
we need a friend. Our God should not be used as a crisis-
management tool. Jesus reminded us also in his words,

"But when ye pray, use not vain repetitions, as the heathen do: for they think that they shall be heard for their much speaking" (Matthew 6:7). All we must do is speak our needs directly to God, and he will answer and deliver us.

On some days, all I could do was to breathe the name of Jesus. One morning after my daughter left the hospital for home, I became very ill and was too weak to call for the nurse's assistant, so there and then I realized that I had to call the only one who is never busy and hears us when we call. These were my exact words: "Jesus, it's you and I alone in this room, and I need your help." Jesus heard my cry and came to my rescue, and I immediately felt better.

It was evident that my case impacted the nursing team as every day I heard positive comments about myself and my room: "Your room is so peaceful" and "I love having you on my caseload." My response to that was, "It's the volume of prayer that goes up in the room daily." Everyone who came to visit took the opportunity to lay hands on me and pray in Jesus's name.

My hospital room slowly transformed into an intercessory prayer room. I heard words such as, "I've never seen someone in pain and still thanking God and praying," "I don't know if you are even aware of the extent of your illness, yet you have maintained a positive and cheerful attitude," and "It's a pleasure to take care of you because you are so grateful and kind." I smiled through the pain, gave God all the glory, and thanked him that I was able to represent him well.

CHAPTER 8

My Vision

I will lift up mine eyes unto the hills, from whence cometh my help. My help cometh from the Lord, which made heaven and earth. (Psalm 121:1–2)

During the night of January 11, 2023, I finally fell asleep after a day filled with pain, medications, and going through the daily routines. And then I had a vision.

I was in a house, lying on a bed all alone. Someone came and took me outside on what appeared to be a stretcher. I was left alone, and people were passing me by and minding their own business; it appeared as if no one cared about me. Suddenly I heard a voice saying, "Look up." I looked up and saw Jesus looking down at me with compassion in his eyes. I have never seen such compassion in anyone's eyes, and right there and then I was reminded of lyrics: "Lord I've seen a world that's dying, wounded by the master of deceit, groping in the darkness haunted by the years of past defeat, but then I see You standing near me, shining with compassion in Your eyes, And I pray, Jesus shine down on me Let your love shine through me in the night."

I gazed into the eyes of Jesus, and then I said, "Jesus, I didn't realize that you loved me so much, but then I saw how you looked at me with compassion, I felt a warmth in my body, and I felt loved." Jesus did not say a word to me, but as I continued to gaze into his eyes, I saw one huge teardrop roll to the side of his eye before coming down slowly and landing on my stomach (the surgery site). I said, "Jesus, you shed a tear for me?" I woke up and felt like a brand-new person; I felt that healing had taken place at the moment the teardrop hit my stomach.

A feeling of happiness and victory came over me, and the nurse noticed a change. She commented, "You look different this morning. Seems like you had a good night's rest." I kept smiling and reliving the vision I had. I shared it with my family members and some friends, and I felt like running, skipping, and jumping for joy because I knew Jesus did it for me.

I am healed! I am healed! Hallelujah! The enemy has lost once again. However, he is never happy when we are victorious, and remember, he never gives up! What did he say in the book of Job? "And the Lord said unto Satan, from whence comest thou? And Satan answered the Lord, and said, from going to and fro in the earth, and from walking up and down in it" (Job 2:2).

CHAPTER 9

Delay Is Not Deny

The day after I had the vision, my sister came into the room with her lunch (chicken quesadilla), and I suddenly felt the urge to ask for a piece of the chicken. Mind you, I had not eaten any solid foods for two months. My sister gladly obliged and gave me the chicken, and I ate a total of four small squares of chicken with no swallowing complications. I then asked for ground meat and ate a couple of pieces from one meatball. This also went down with no complications. It was a hallelujah moment for my sister and me.

My sister was so excited that she called some family members and shared the good news. The nurse came in to give me my scheduled medications, and my sister excitedly informed her that I had eaten without feeling nauseated. News of my eating circulated, and I received positive encouragement and applause from the care team. My determination to go home without the TPN tube motivated me to push and try harder.

Despite my valiant effort and my daily increase in intake, the medical team still felt that I needed support through TPN as my blood work was still abnormal. My body had experienced trauma and needed nutrients to complete its repair.

Four days after I began eating, I was medically cleared to return home with the TPN tube and in-home nursing services. I experienced mixed feelings when this information was relayed to me. I wanted to go home but not with any adaptive devices.

An insurance discrepancy caused a delay in finalizing the discharge paperwork; however, we know the scripture that states, "And we know that all things work together for good to them that love God, to them who are the called according to his purpose" (Romans 8:28). The case manager came to my room to update me on what was causing the delay. I was not fully engaged in the discussion as I believed that this delay would be for my good as the plan of God unfolded.

My intake and output were now monitored with intensity, and although my intake had increased, I was still receiving twenty-four-hour TPN. I continued to talk to God to ask him to give me a better appetite so that I could consume nutrient-rich foods that would be beneficial to my body. Nurses drew blood two to three times daily, and my levels were closely monitored.

As the nursing team went over the results with me, my faith in God increased. I continued to hold onto his promises that he would never leave me nor forsake me. My strength was being renewed, and my determination to return home was first and foremost on my mind. I knew that prayers were going up for me every moment of the day.

Two days before my discharge, the team of OR surgeons came to my room early in the morning for their usual check-in. One of the surgeons said, "How are you feeling today?" I answered that I was feeling good now. He then said, "If I should ask you to make a wish, what would it be?" Without hesitation, I said, "My wish is to be discharged home to my family without the aid of this TPN or any home-nursing services."

The surgeon validated my feelings, stating, "I totally understand; however, the head surgeon has to make that final decision." I felt hopeful then, and somehow, I knew I would be discharged without the TPN. Later that day, the head surgeon came to my room and discussed my progress and his reservations concerning in-home TPN care and support.

CHAPTER 10

The Work Must Be Completed

TPN was no longer an option in my book, for I know that my God always finishes the work that he starts. He said, "Lo. I am with you always, even unto the end of the world. Amen" (Matthew 28:20). The twenty-four-hour TPN feeding was reduced to twelve hours (that's progress)! The following morning, I received another bit of good news: "The doctor has discontinued your TPN tube; therefore, the line will be removed before you leave for home."

Yes! Thank you, Jesus, for coming through for me once again. I was grinning from ear to ear, and I could hardly contain my excitement. It was time to worship! Progress! Victory! Suddenly there seemed to be more than twenty-four hours in the day as everything appeared to have slowed down. The thought of going home became more intense, and I felt that the only reason I wasn't discharged that day was that it was a public holiday, Dr. Martin Luther King Jr. Day.

I believe that was the very best day for me at the hospital. My spirit soared high, and I felt calm and relaxed, especially since I was able to read the encouraging texts that came in from my immediate and church family. One person wrote, "But they that wait upon the Lord shall renew their strength; they shall mount up with wings as eagles; they shall run, and not be weary; and they shall walk, and not faint" (Isaiah 40:31). Immediately this song dropped in my spirit:

> Hold on my child joy comes in the morning, weeping only last for the night, hold on my child joy comes in the morning, the darkest hour means dawn is just in sight.

It had been eighteen days since I was hospitalized, and this was the day that I would soar like an eagle. I was going home without the TPN. The OR team took their final walk to my room, and the conversation was very meaningful. One of the surgeons looked at me and stated, "Over the past two days I noticed how you changed right before my eyes, and I like what I am seeing."

The surgeon hinted that I might be discharged on that day; however, he reminded me that once again the head surgeon would make the final decision. After the team of surgeons left the room, I immediately called home and told my husband to be prepared to pick me up because I would be discharged. The head surgeon came shortly, and we went over the preliminaries, including his decision to have the TPN line removed.

Hallelujah! I was going home without the assistive device or nursing services! Hallelujah! I believe that, at that moment, I was the happiest person in the entire hospital. What a mighty God we serve! Jesus had done it again! He came through for me, and the impossible was made possible through Jesus Christ.

CONCLUSION

Time to Say Goodbye

The process of removing the TPN line was the final major hurdle to clear before leaving the hospital. The nurses provided step-by-step details as to how the line would be removed. I listened attentively, and when asked if I was ready, I boldly said, "As ready as can be!" I owe it all to Jesus because he was with me every step of the way, thus allowing me to experience peace and calmness through even the most grueling experiences.

"Thou wilt keep him in perfect peace, whose mind is stayed on thee: because he trusteth in thee" (Isaiah 26:3). The line was removed, and the nurse reviewed the discharge instructions with me. I said my final goodbyes and thank yous to the phenomenal team of caregivers on East Tower 8.

In retrospect, I am convinced that many lives were touched and impacted through my being a patient at that hospital, as throughout my sickness I represented Jesus well. I was respectful and thankful to all my caregivers and always gave a smile as I received care.

My continual refrain of "Thank you, Jesus" was noted, and as I said earlier, one of my nurses remarked, "I have never seen someone in pain and thanking Jesus."

I am cognizant of the fact that, as children of God, we must let our lights shine wherever we go to help those who are groping in the darkness. "Let your light so shine before men, that they may see your good works, and glorify your Father which is in heaven" (Matthew 5:16). Irrespective of the situations or circumstances, we should be mindful of our actions. "Do all things without murmurings and disputing's: that ye may be blameless and harmless, the sons of God, without rebuke, in the midst of a crooked and perverse nation, among whom ye shine as lights in the world" (Philippians 2:14–15).

You are never alone! Jesus is with you. Sometimes in the midnight hour, when no one is around and fear comes your way, be reminded that Jesus is with you. Pray earnestly and consistently while you have the chance. When sickness rocks your body, you may not have the strength to pray; however, rest assured that the prayers that are "in storage" for you will be released in the time of need.

The battle was still raging even after my discharge from the hospital and I experienced several days of medical challenges, but by this time my strength and faith had increased to the point where I denounced the false evidence (a preaching topic by one of my ministers). He illustrated the story of Joseph with a coat that had what appeared to be human blood on it and declared that was false evidence.

I jumped up from the couch and began to declare complete healing over my life, and the following week I was able to go back to church for the first time in three months. Thank you, Jesus, for never leaving me alone!

-The End-

ABOUT THE AUTHOR

 Tenssie Veronica Ramsay, MS, NCC, LPC, is a Licensed Professional Counselor with the state of Connecticut. She was born in a quaint district called Linstead in the parish of St. Catherine, Jamaica, West Indies. She graduated from Dinthill Technical High School in Jamaica and several other tertiary institutions prior to migrating to the United States of America.

She holds an associate's degree in health care administration and a bachelor of science in health care administration from the University of Phoenix; a master of science from the University of Bridgeport; and a professional counselor license through the Connecticut Department of Health.

She owns her private practice, CareWings Counseling LLC, in Bridgeport, Connecticut, where she provides service to a wide cross-section of the population in Bridgeport and surrounding cities. She sings on the praise and worship team at church and is also a Sunday schoolteacher.

She is married to Collie A. Ramsay and has three awesome adult children: Natasha, Alwyain, and Joshua.

Printed in the United States
by Baker & Taylor Publisher Services